You will show me the path
to life, abounding joy in
Your presence, the delights
at Your right hand forever.
Psalm 16:11

The intent and
purpose of this volume is to
give you faith, hope and
inspiration. Hopefully it will help bring
peace and tranquility into your life. May
it be a reminder of God's love, guidance
and His many blessings.

Our publications help to support our work
for needy children in over 130 countries
around the world. Through our
programs, thousands of children are
fed, clothed, educated, sheltered
and given the opportunity to
live decent lives.

Salesian Missions wishes to extend special thanks and gratitude to ou
generous poet friends and to the publishers who have given us permission to repris
material included in this book. Every effort has been made to give prop
acknowledgments. Any omissions or errors are deeply regretted, and the publisher, upc
notification, will be pleased to make the necessary corrections in subsequent editions

Cover photo: © Fotosearch/Mountain in Waterton National Park Alberta

First Edition Printed in the U.S.A. by Concord Litho, Concord, NH 03301.

Passages of Peace
from the
Salesian Collection

Compiled and Edited
by Jennifer Grimaldi

Illustrated by
Paul Scully, Bob Pantelone,
Russell Bushée, Geraldine Aikman,
Frank Massa, Dorian Remine,
Terrie Meider, and Robert VanSteinburg

Contents

Sustain me by Your promise that I may
live; do not disappoint me in my hope.
Help me, that I may be safe and ever
delight in Your statutes.
Psalms 119:116, 117

The Promise of Spring

Sunshine and a robin's song –
Sweet promise that it won't be long
Before the earth bursts into bloom.
Oh anxious heart, it will be soon
That daffodils defy the chill
And nod upon the barren hill,
Tender leaves unfold again
After a gentle April rain.
And blossoms pink and blossoms white
Adorn the trees, a sheer delight.
Little lambs clad in white fleece
Frolic in the gentle breeze.
And children laugh and run and play
Without a care, all through the day.
It won't be long, wait patiently –
Soon every heart makes melody,
And heeds the sunshine's beckoning call
To join the fun 'til shadows fall.

Regina Wiencek

Let Your love come to me,
Lord, salvation in accord
with Your promise.
Psalm 119:41

The hay appeareth, and the tender grass showeth itself, and herbs of the mountains are gathered.
Proverbs 27:25

8

The Display of Springtide

I see a verdant meadow,
The birds are on the wing.
A little girl's a-swinging
Down on the old tree's swing.

The gardeners are gardening –
This is the season's chore.
The bees are getting busy –
They're buzzing 'round the door.

The peepers in yon woodland
Now sound their mating call.
Buds are turning into leaves
On trees both small and tall.

The dandelions are popping
In yards, on hillsides, too;
After Winter's dusting time,
God's springtide blooms anew.

Loise Pinkerton Fritz

Thank You

Lord, I thank You
For the trials I face,
For all Your love
And constant grace.
Through the trials
You help me grow
And reach out to
Help others know
All about Your
Unfailing love,
As You freely bless us
From Your throne above.
Thank You for the guidance
Each and every day,
That never fails to bless me
Much more than I can say.

Dona M. Maroney

My eyes grow dim from trouble.
All day I call on You, Lord; I
stretch out my hands to You.
Psalm 88:10

Who Can Doubt He Cares?

We can sense God in the morning
As we breathe the fresh, clean air,
In the country where the dewdrops
Cling to roses soft and fair.
We can sense God at noon
As we stroll amid the garden,
Viewing yellow buttercups,
Assured our sins are pardoned.
We can sense God in the evening
When morning glories fold.
Just to catch a glimpse of the sunset –
God's love revealed so bold!

We can sense God at night
When darkness overtakes,
Trusting in His everlasting love –
Sweet peace when we awake.
God tenderly watches o'er us…
Who can doubt He cares
When each hour ticks a miracle
Bursting forth 'most everywhere?

Linda C. Grazulis

Cast all your worries upon Him
because He cares for you.
1 Peter 5:7

The Lord Has Given

The Lord has given us a new day,
A chance to do some good,
To share His precious gift of life,
As all His children should.
A chance to praise His Holy Name,
A chance to give Him laud;
A gracious, kind Creator,
Our wise and loving God.

The Lord has given us a new way
To share His joy with man –
A Son to pave a righteous path
That follows His own plan,
That through His ministry on earth
Attained redemption for His own,
That we might lay our crown of life
Before His holy throne.

Nancy Watson Dodrill

*But when you have eaten your
fill, you must bless the Lord,
Your God, for the good
country He has given you.*
Deuteronomy 8:10

Prayer Requests

Lord, I come to You with prayer requests,
For I know You always know what's best.
The plans I make I leave with You
That You may change them if You choose.
And loved ones who have lost their way
Will come back to You, dear Lord, I pray.
An answer from You means so much,
For those who need Your healing touch.
And those who fear may have Your peace –
Their faith in You to be complete.
Now use me, Lord, that I might do
Whatever it is You want me to,
And whatever I do, wherever I go,
Your love to others help me to show.

Millie Torzilli

Grant what is in your heart,
fulfill your every plan.
Psalm 20:5

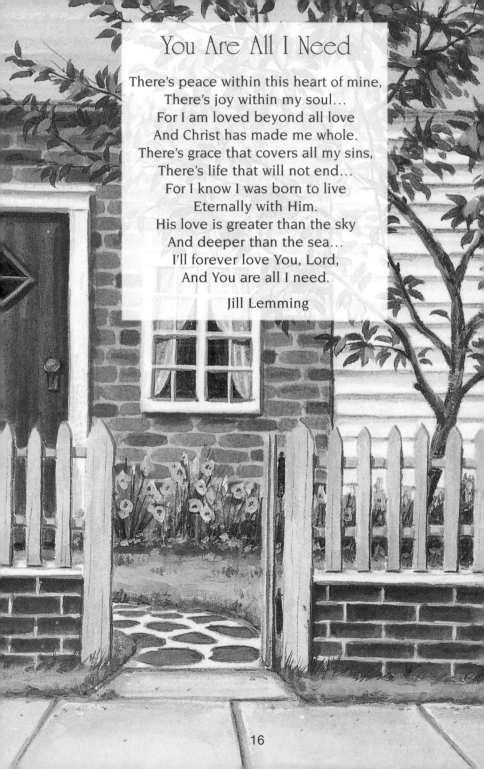

You Are All I Need

There's peace within this heart of mine,
There's joy within my soul…
For I am loved beyond all love
And Christ has made me whole.
There's grace that covers all my sins,
There's life that will not end…
For I know I was born to live
Eternally with Him.
His love is greater than the sky
And deeper than the sea…
I'll forever love You, Lord,
And You are all I need.

Jill Lemming

Another Door Opens

To those who will listen
Through shadows of time,
His words speak of goodness,
Of love, so sublime.
Through trials on earth that
Include pain and tears,
The Lord gives us courage...
Erases all fears.
And if one door closes,
We may feel distress,
But the next open door
May bring true happiness.
Let us walk by His side,
Surrounded by light,
Though today may be weary...
Tomorrow will be bright.

Angie Monnens

Ask and it will be given to
you; seek and you will
find; knock and the door
will be opened to you.
Matthew 7:7

Giving Thanks

Thank You, God, for roses red
And for rustling Autumn leaves,
The hummingbird, every morning glory,
And for the nests wee robins weave.
Thank You, God, for tiny things –
Buzzing bees, swift butterflies.
The crocus following Winter's blast
Removes a weary sigh.
Thank You, God, for daffodils
'Cause they teach us how to shine,
The freshly painted garden trellis
And lush grapes strung on the vine.
Thank You, God, for pastures green
And for the babbling of a brook,
For mossy stumps and field mushrooms –
Just take some time to look.

Thank You, God, for humble smiles
Easing shadows of despair,
Offered by a kindly stranger
Or a friend who truly cares.
Mostly, God, we thank Thee
For children oh, so small,
They teach us how to laugh again –
The greatest gift of all.

Linda C. Grazulis

*Giving thanks always and
for everything in the name
of our Lord, Jesus Christ,
to God the Father.*
Ephesians 5:20

Go Tell Someone

Go tell the world of the wondrous deeds
That Jesus Christ has done;
Tell of His mighty miracles
And deep love for everyone.
Go tell someone that Jesus reigns
And we have living proof;
Go tell someone that Jesus saves
And He's the life and truth.
Go spread the news of our Lord;
Go tell someone each day.
With Jesus we have victory
Because He is the way!

Nell Ford Hann

I'll Be Okay

I'll be okay – my Jesus loves me;
I'll be okay – my Jesus cares.
He is my Lord, my blessed Savior –
He answers all my prayers.

Troubles may come, but I'll recover;
My faith in His word prevails.
Jesus restores me, gives me courage –
His love and mercy never fails.

I'll be okay and naught can hurt me;
Jesus is with me every day.
He is protecting – He is my lifeline –
There is no doubt I'll be okay.

Jesus is there – He walks beside me;
He gives me strength, He leads my way.
I'm not alone, His spirit guides me –
There is no doubt I'll be okay.

Patience Allison Hartbauer

*For the spirit of God has
made me, the breath of the
Almighty keeps me alive.
Job 33:4*

21

You Can't Argue With the Wind

You can't argue with the wind
Or control the ocean tide.
Some things are beyond your power,
Too big, too deep, too wide.

So put things in perspective;
See how they measure up –
Just a drop in the bucket
Or an overflowing cup?

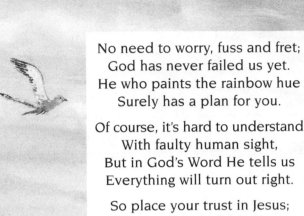

No need to worry, fuss and fret;
God has never failed us yet.
He who paints the rainbow hue
Surely has a plan for you.

Of course, it's hard to understand
With faulty human sight,
But in God's Word He tells us
Everything will turn out right.

So place your trust in Jesus;
Turn loose of doubt and fear.
All is well – no matter what –
And Heaven's very near!

Elaine Hardt

New Hope

There's a new hope dawning with the day,
As flowers open their eyes.
There's a new faith spurning doubt away,
As glory shines beyond the skies.
There's a new satisfaction, a peacefulness,
As love-ones linger near.
There's a new heartfelt action, a prayerfulness,
When the birds echo our cheer.

There's a new joy felt in a service of love,
As we help those in need.
There's a new kind of happiness felt above
When we plant God's precious seed.
There's a new kind of morning after the night,
As we behold the sun's jeweled ray.
There's a new hope dawning, new faith in sight,
And it starts anew today.

Janice George

*Lead us back to You,
O Lord, that we may be
restored: give us anew such
days as we had of old.*
Lamentations 5:21

Loving Master

We know that earthly burdens
Must surely come our way,
But God can make them lighter
If we go to Him and pray.
He will give us needed strength
To overcome our fears
And will grant us understanding
In every plea He hears.
Life is so much easier
When we place our faith in God
And make Him our loving Master
As we walk this earthly sod.

Shirley Hile Powell

Faith, Trust, Hope

God is our constant Savior,
He cares for you and me;
A guiding, loving Father,
We feel but cannot see.

He knows our wants and needs,
Answers heartfelt prayer;
In His own way, He reaches out,
To let us know He's there.

He gives us strength to meet our trials,
Faith we need to cope,
Patience and trust day by day,
And the miracle of hope.

Ruth Moyer Gilmour

*Trust God and He will help
you; make straight your
ways and hope in Him.*
Sirach 2:6

The Master's Hand

I see Him in the morning sun
That golden tips the trees.
I hear Him in the rippling stream
In soft, sweet evening breeze…

In the shining silver moon,
On the lake at midnight bright,
When night birds sound a winsome call,
Frog choirs salute the night…

The splendor of His hand
In flaming leaves of Fall,
Rosy apples, pumpkins bright
Cornstalks standing tall…

In a snowflake's gentle flight,
Covering all throughout the night,
Then dawn reveals a dazzling scene,
Pristine pure, silent and serene.

Some people claim this can't be planned –
And cannot conceive the Master's hand.
God, give them the hearts to see
In all Your creativity.

Leah Zink

*The heavens belong to
the Lord, but the earth
is given to us.*
Psalm 115:16

At dawn let me hear of Your kindness, for in You I trust. Show me the path I should walk, for to You I entrust my life.

Psalm 143:8

Letting Go

I see the sadness in your eyes
And sense the inner pain;
I know you feel a hopelessness
And cry for help in vain.
I long to hold you close and say,
"Let go, let go your fears;
Let God become your faithful friend
And dry away your tears.
Release your doubts and trust in Him
To gently show the way,
Be grateful with a humble heart
And take the time to pray.
If this you do, releasing self
With simple faith and love,
He'll fill your heart with new-found joy
And bless you from above."

Vi B. Chevalier

When I am afraid, in
You I place my trust.
Psalm 56:4

The Splendor of Autumn

The splendor of Autumn
Blesses my heart,
As the October leaves
Become works of art.

The wonders of Nature
Set hillsides aglow
From the mountains above
To valleys below.

No artists' pallet
Forms colors like these
When the splendor of Autumn
Transforms the trees.

Such beauty is fleeting
And soon fades away,
But sweet memories linger
On cold Winter days.

The wonders of God
Are living works of art
When the splendor of Autumn
Blesses my heart.

Clay Harrison

He maketh the storm a calm, so that the waves there of are still.
Psalm 107:29

God's Protective Arm

I face each day with trust in Thee
That they that seek Your face shall be
Enveloped by Your protective arm
That calms the storm and keeps from harm.
I know you'll comfort those who mourn
With tender love to heal hearts so torn;
They'll be consoled and reasurred
That You, my Lord, will keep Your word.
There is a covenant that He made
That promises hope and love and aid
To those who pray an ernest prayer
That You will keep them in Your care.

Beverly Huff

Children, let us love not in word or speech
but in deed and truth. Now this is how we
shall know that we belong to the truth and
reassure our hearts before Him.
1 John 3:18,19

Kindness

Do you see someone discouraged,
Needing a bit of cheer today?
Then go on, share the Lord,
Giving them hope along the way.
Kindness has God-given power
To uplift one's burden and care.
'Tis a candle in their dark night,
Dispersing love's light here and there.

Kindness loans strength to the weary,
Rekindling that flame flick'ring low.
It beams sunshine to the dreary
And on the face an afterglow.
Kindness is casting out God's bread,
For it shall come back to us one day.
Someday we may need to be fed
And in kindness, someone will pray.

Nancy Sousley

Whispers

When the valley of the shadow
Leads us to despair,
Take comfort in the certitude
That He is always there.

It is a mystic sound
Like whispers on the air;
A gentle voice that says,
"I'm listening and I care."

In our time of want,
No sorrow is too small.
When we pray for help,
There's an answer to our call.

No one ever walks alone,
For He does understand;
You will hear Him whisper,
"Come and take My hand."

C. David Hay

*Yet I am always with You; You
take hold of my right hand.*
Psalm 73:23

Peace of Mind

When thoughts like leaves scatter about,
Because my mind is filled with doubt,
Remind me, Lord, to think things through –
Remind me, Lord, to wait for You.
When all contentment slips away,
Because my mind begins to stray,
Relieve me, Lord, from my concerns –
Receive me, Lord, so peace returns.
Whenever thoughts roll through my mind,
Because Your peace is hard to find,
Show me, Lord, a better way –
Show me, Lord, that it's okay.

When fear and worry take their toll,
Dragging down my struggling soul,
Teach me, Lord, to let things go –
Teach me, Lord, so I can grow.
Before my mind turns to despair,
Believing You have gone somewhere,
Help me see You in the flowers –
Help me see Your silent power.
Before my spirit goes astray,
Lost without hope and can't find my way,
Guide me, Lord, to seek Your face –
Guide me, Lord, to thoughts of grace.

John Zurn

Tell Them Today

Is there someone needing a word of cheer
Who is living with a heavy heart?
Perhaps only you have the words he needs…
Words of comfort just you can impart.
We know there are those who want to hear
Their burdens need not be endured alone.
That we will be there through thick and thin,
For this is the way that love is sown.
Be it family member, friend, or neighbor,
Or a stranger met along the way,
They all could use an encouraging word;
Don't wait 'til later… tell them today.

M. Elaine Fowser

Many Blessings

Thank You for so many tranquil moments,
And the many moments of reflection;
Moments that have inspired,
Others that gave direction.

Thank You for the time to read the Word
And listen closely to Your voice;
Loving, precious times
That were often times of choice.

Thank You for the times of struggle
And the times of bliss;
The difficult, troubling times,
The times of tenderness.

Thank You for the legacy of life
You laid before my feet;
For each and every blessing,
The bitter and the sweet.

Barbara Joan Million

*Then the Lord looked upon the earth,
and filled it with His blessings.*
Sirach 16:27

Comfort in Tears

Every teardrop weeping out
Is wiped away with love.
God blots the tears in special ways
With His comfort from above.
When you weep your tears of woe
And sadness, grief and pain,
God comes with healing that's divine,
Giving sunshine where once was rain.

Carol Zileski

Never Doubt

God wipes away our tears
And well He understands.
He's seen us as we are;
He holds us in His hands.

He knows when we try
To do our very best;
He blesses us for that,
So put all doubts to rest.

He sees all things so well;
He knows what we're about.
So place your hand in His
And never, never doubt.

Take your sorrows and your tears
And give Him all of them.
Our hurts He then will mend
If we place our trust in Him.

Bernice Laux

*He did not doubt God's promise in
unbelief; rather, he was empowered
by faith and gave glory to God.*
Romans 4:20

There is an appointed time for everything, and a time for every affair under the heavens.
Ecclesiastes 3:1

In His Time

Do you know that He carries you?
You are one of His lambs.
And He comforts and guides you
With His strong, loving hands.

He never grows weary,
Nor will He turn you away.
He knows all your problems,
And gives grace for each day.

As you've walked through dark valleys,
He has provided the light for you.
Have you given Him praise
For the trials He's seen you through?

Look up to Him now and give Him thanks;
He is working out His plan.
Although today your load seems heavy,
In His time, you'll understand.

Theo Cusato

*But I pray to You, Lord, for the
time of Your favor. God, in Your
great kindness answer me with
Your constant help.*
Psalm 69:14

Who Is God?

Who is God, my weary soul demands,
Is He present in this day?
Does He see my stumbling footsteps?
Can He stop to show the way?
Does He understand my longings,
Can He sense my deepest needs?
Can He pause to render comfort,
Will He soon sow loving seeds?
Does He want me, does He need me,
Is there work for me to do?
Sometimes the doubts are many,
The certainties all too few.
But when at last, in prayer, I rest
At the closing of each day,
He softly whispers, "Fear thou not.
I am with you, I am the way."

Loretta Garing

Each and Every Person

Each and every person
Has a very special place,
Which fulfills a special mission
And is touched by love and grace...

Each and every person
Fills a very special role,
Which reveals a special talent
That lies deep within the soul...

Each and every person
Plays a very special part,
Which portrays a special calling
And lives within the heart!

Hope C. Oberhelman

*To this end, we always pray for you,
that our God may make you worthy
of His calling and powerfully bring
to fulfillment every good purpose
and every effort of faith.*
2 Thessalonians 1:11

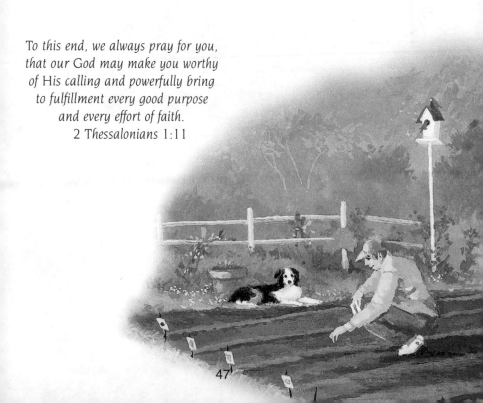

47

Perfect Rest in Jesus

I was busy in the garden
Raking, hoeing, shoveling;
It was in the morning hours
In the early time of Spring.
Through the air the birds were winging,
Chirping, singing merrily,
While out yon in the meadow,
Cattle grazed contentedly.
When several hours passed me by,
I was seeking some sweet rest,
So I leaned upon my shovel
'Til I got my second breath.

While leaning on the shovel there,
In the early part of day,
My thoughts were wending heavenward
While quietly I prayed:
"We can lean upon a shovel
For a bit of breathing time,
But it's when we lean on You, Lord,
That a perfect rest we'll find."

Loise Pinkerton Fritz

49

Renew my heart each day, dear Lord.
Remove sin's heavy load.
Break down the idols I've built inside
And make it Your abode.

Renew my strength each day, dear Lord.
Let me find power within.
Give me the wit to do Thy will
And victory over sin.

Renew my faith each day, dear Lord,
With the freshness of the rain.
May I spring forth like daffodils
And proclaim Your Holy Name.

Janice George

You Can Do Anything

You can do anything if you believe!
If you take Christ's hand you then will receive
Pure peace and calm and love, He'll supply
Courage and hope that you cannot deny.
See yourself perfect and whole everyday;
Don't let the negative stand in your way.
With faith of a child you honestly know
Opportunity is yours to strengthen and grow.
Believe every second you always have hope,
Strength to endure and ability to cope.
But far beyond this you'll find peace of mind,
If you trust in the Lord and the answers you'll find.
Believe you can do anything – let this be your story,
With God as your Kingdom, your Power, and your Glory.

Edna Louise Gilbert

*Therefore I tell you, all that you ask
for in prayer, believe that you will
receive it and it shall be yours.*
Mark 11:24

Nature's Alarm Clock

Nature's alarm is ringing;
I wonder how it knows
To tell the seeds beneath the soil
It's time to wake and grow?

All Winter, silent, they have lain
Beneath the snow at rest;
Content to be just where they were,
Against the earth's warm breast.

But now they hear the summons
That it's time to rise and shine;
To greet them in my garden
Is a springtime joy of mine.

Each Spring I wait with longing
For this moment to arrive;
To see them first come peeking through
Makes my spirit come alive…

For I count them as a message
That God has sent my way
To restore me with the promise
Of His love this springtime day.

Don Beckman

53

I, the Creator, who gave them life.
Peace, peace to the far and the near,
says the Lord; and I will heal them.
Isaiah 57:19

Healing Power

God never allows a burden
Too difficult to bear.
All things are for a purpose
And God keeps us in His care.

We thank God for His grace;
His love is always there.
And He forgives, as we forgive.
God's presence – we declare.

All healing power God offers.
Do not doubt or fear –
Just ask our Lord to help you.
The Bible makes it clear.

God listens as we pray;
He is our guiding light.
Trust in God's power and love
And all things will turn out right.

Edna Massimilla

Heal me, Lord, that I may be
healed; save me, that I may be
saved, for it is You whom I praise.
Jeremiah 17:14

Look Up

I stumbled down a rocky road,
My head hung low in pain.
My heart did ache from such a load.
I saw no sunshine, only rain.
Then came a whisper on the wind,
So gently did it blow,
And looking up I found a Friend
Who banished all my woe.

Ruth Gillis

In Farewell

How few of us travel together
Life's same roadways for long?
For each, through some unseen guidance,
Choose paths that are right or wrong.

And none of us know at what instant
Our present highway ends,
With another to take us farther
From the old, familiar friends.

But each, with searching and longing,
Are grateful for those we find
With the hands of friendship offered
And hearts that are true and kind!

So here, at another crossroad,
Going our separate ways,
Let us wish each other safe travels
And bright and happier days!

John C. Bonser

*"Fear not, beloved, you are safe;
take courage and be strong."*
Daniel 10:19

Green Pastures

He never said we'd always have
Green pastures, sweet with rain.
He only said He'd walk with us
Through valleys, deep with pain.

He never promised stoneless paths
By waters, always still,
But told us, with His rod and staff,
He'd help us past the hill.

Sometimes our paths are weary when
We're burdened down with care,
But He will hold our hands in His,
With faith, we'll meet Him there.

We're told to always trust in Him,
For in His strength we'll find
A solace and a comfort with
A peaceful heart and mind.

We know there always will be hills
With valleys in between,
But be assured, someday we'll dwell
In pastures that are green.

Mary Dalton Crump

*He ranges the mountains for
pasture, and seeks out every
patch of green.*
Job 39:8

What Really Counts

Things that really count
Are those you cannot see,
Like love and happy feelings,
And blessed harmony…

Thoughts that you are thinking,
Prayers you say at night,
And God who's always with you
To help you do things right.

Ruth Moyer Gilmour

You Can Do It!

You can succeed if you believe –
Just reach out and persevere.
Place your goals in God's out-stretched hands
For He knows which way to steer.

With every struggle be optimistic
And eventually you'll see
That with each blow stronger you'll grow
From an acorn to a towering tree!

Sometimes you'll need to cast an anchor
To pause and meditate.
It's during these times our God refines,
So don't worry about your fate!

Have faith in God and you can do it,
Even though dreams seem destined to fail.
Trust God when those nasty storm clouds gather
To make you a much stronger sail!

Linda C. Grazulis

*Be strong and take heart, all
you who hope in the Lord.
Psalm 31:25*

Passage to Peace

Somewhere in the darkened night,
Our souls cry in despair,
An empty, aimless vessel
In need of hope and prayer.

Our shallow souls beg closure,
Our hearts are broken, lost,
But God would tend our needs –
Save us – at any cost.

His love is in our friendships,
In calmed or stormy seas.
His love pervades our beings –
It always strengthens me.

May His love give you courage
And the will to fight
Your fears of the darkness,
The strangers in the night.

May His love give you guidance
To navigate a course,
To sail the roughest waters,
To know your strongest force.

May you embrace His passion
Then share from deep within
Your joy that's ever-present
Because… you're trusting Him.

Janice M. Cortis

If I fly with the wings of dawn and alight beyond the sea. Even there Your hand will guide me, Your right hand hold me fast.
Psalm 139:9,10

Wild Geese

I saw a chain of birds today,
A necklace in the sky,
Synchronized, in unison…
The wild geese passing by.

I looked up at the blessing,
Your gift for tired eyes.
I never seem to get my fill
Of wild geese in the skies.

I always gaze in wonder,
In joy and pure delight,
Whenever I'm alerted
To the wild geese in flight.

My eyes drink of the blessing
And follow them in flight
Until they disappear from view,
No longer in my sight.

And yet, I feel a sense of peace
Long after they are gone…
Anointed by the blessing,
The moment lingers on.

Dolores Dahl

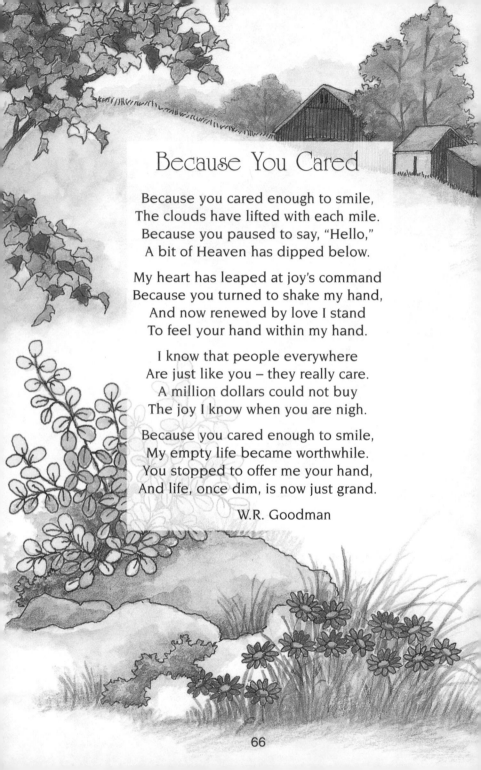

Because You Cared

Because you cared enough to smile,
The clouds have lifted with each mile.
Because you paused to say, "Hello,"
A bit of Heaven has dipped below.

My heart has leaped at joy's command
Because you turned to shake my hand,
And now renewed by love I stand
To feel your hand within my hand.

I know that people everywhere
Are just like you – they really care.
A million dollars could not buy
The joy I know when you are nigh.

Because you cared enough to smile,
My empty life became worthwhile.
You stopped to offer me your hand,
And life, once dim, is now just grand.

W.R. Goodman

Golden Season

Dear Lord, I'm growing older.
May I treasure every day
And walk with a grateful heart
With You leading the way.
For those who have a need.
Help me to be worthy
By thoughtful act or deed.
Make me warm and mellow,
Patient, true and kind.
Let me seek out learning
For a busy, active mind.
Guide me in my Autumn,
Bless these years with cheer,
For my Winter fast approaches
And time becomes so dear.
Grant me youthful vision,
Make simple joys my quest,
So that the Golden Season
Will prove to be my best!

Virginia Borman Grimmer

*For the age that is honorable comes not
with the passing of time, nor can it be
measured in terms of years.*
Wisdom 4:8

There Is Beauty

There is beauty in the sunset,
The multi-colors of the sky,
In the silhouette of birds on wing
As they go flying by.
There is beauty in God's paint brush
As He paints on azure blue –
Colors that no man can name,
So vivid, clear, and true.

There is beauty in the night bird's song
That falls in harmony
With peepers from the distant pond
And a cricket's jamboree.
There is beauty in the lullaby
Of softly falling rain –
Its tattoo rends a rhythm's beat
Within its moist refrain.

There is beauty in the fragrance
Of the honeysuckle vine,
The bittersweet ambrosia
With a bouquet of fine wine.
There is beauty in the aroma
Of grass that's freshly mown,
Or the turning of the soil
Soon after seeds are sown.

Beauty is the miracle
We experience with eye and ear.
The wonder of all of our senses
On an evening calm and clear.
There would be no greater sorrow,
No burden man could lift,
To find, with deep-felt heartbreak,
With the loss of such a gift.

Nancy Watson Dodrill

Oh, Comfort Me!

Come now, my Lord, and comfort me –
The lightless night is here.
Oh, take my hand and chase away
The shadowed wings of fear!

Now while I walk the dark unknown,
Be ever close and near.
Oh, comfort me, love of my life,
My Jesus, sweet and dear!

Kate Watkins Furman

Give Me Your Strength

Lord, give me Your strength
When troubles come my way;
I look to You for courage
To make it through the day.

Give strength that brings a victory
To triumph over trials,
To turn each sadness into joy
And face life with a smile.

I'll hide Thy Word within my heart
As I plant it fresh each day
And water it with praise
Each time I thank and pray.

That inner strength will take me through
No matter what's to be.
If You are walking by my side,
I'll walk in victory.

Helen Gleason

*Lord, You are the strength of
Your people, the saving refuge
of Your anointed King.*
Psalm 28:8

On Mountains High

On mountains high on days like this,
My spirit soars above,
Above the valley of the shadow
To God's redeeming love.

On mountains high where eagles nest,
I feel so close to God,
For here there is a quiet rest
Above the trodden sod.

On mountains high, the clouds pass by,
Close enough to touch.
These are the special moments
That inspire us so much.

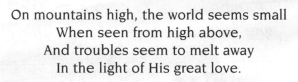

On mountains high, the world seems small
When seen from high above,
And troubles seem to melt away
In the light of His great love.

When molehills become mountains
We think we cannot climb,
We reach the top with faith renewed
And life begins to rhyme.

God meets us on the mountaintop
And in the valley too,
And we will never be the same
When He comes into view!

Clay Harrison

May the God of hope fill you with all joy and peace in believing, so that you may abound in hope by the power of the Holy Spirit.
Romans 15:13

His Lovelight

The lovelight of God shines down on me
All throughout the day,
And in my darkest hour, I see
Its very brightest ray.
It lifts me out of deep despair
Into His world, free from care,
And there I find joy, contentment and peace,
When all of my burdens to Him I release.

His lovelight sustains my very soul
And I'm happy to be in His tender control.
He keeps my steps from going astray
When He holds my hand and leads the way.
Along the banks of the rivers of life,
He keeps me safe through storms and strife.
Through valleys green, o'er meadows fair,
His lovelight keeps shining everywhere.

Lou Ella Cullipher

*Rise up in splendor! Your
light has come, the glory of
the Lord shines upon you.*
Isaiah 60:1

A Bridge to God

Help me, God, to always be
A bridge of hope and love for Thee.
Help me share, as best I can,
Your holy Word with my fellow man.

Help me lead a life that's true,
Inspire a soul in search of You.
Help me show how much I care
To those who have a cross to bear.

Help me be a beam of light
When sorrows turn day into night.
Help me give a helping hand
To those who seek to understand.

Help me heal a hurting heart
And precious peace and joy impart.
Help me, God, to always be
A bridge of hope and love for Thee.

Vi B. Chevalier

Majesty

Dear God, I hear Your mighty voice
As rain begins to fall
And thunder rumbles to the earth
And birds respond in call.

Dear God, I hear Your mighty voice
As wind blows long and shrill,
As Winter sleet coats every tree
Upon the stormy hill.

Dear God, I hear Your mighty voice
As I survey the sea –
The power, the calm, the reverence –
Your glory – majesty!

Hazel M. Blough

Testament

Life is an open book,
A page turned every day.
We alone determine
What the story is to say.

Some are tales of triumph,
Others wrought with woe.
All have the same beginning –
The end we do not know.

Be the novel great or small,
The paper is the same.
Its content is the measure
Not the cover or the name.

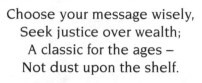

Choose your message wisely,
Seek justice over wealth;
A classic for the ages –
Not dust upon the shelf.

When comes the final chapter
And the pen is laid to rest,
May God in final judgement say
He knows we tried to write our best.

C. David Hay

God's Undying Love

Whenever you are sick and discouraged
And everything seems to go wrong;
Put your hand in the hand of the Savior,
The hands that are loving, but strong.
He promised us "strength for the weary;"
He promised His undying love.
So, if you think you can't take anymore,
Turn your eyes to the Father above.

Helen Ruth Ashton

Thank You, Lord

I marvel at the splendor that surrounds me,
The beauty that expands from sky to sea.
Oh God, how can I ever start to thank You
For all the wondrous things You've given me?

I thank You, Lord, for trees that grace the woodlands,
For every growing thing that's bright and fair,
For mountains high and every golden meadow.
'Cause wherever there is beauty You are there.

I see the stars, I feel the sun –
Your majesty spreads far and wide.
I've seen the light, I feel Your love –
I am safe because I know You're at my side.

I thank You, Lord, for many countless blessings,
For promises and answers to my prayers.
I never want to fear because I know You love me,
Dearest Lord, because I know You truly care.

Patience Allison Hartbauer

*We thank You, God, we give
thanks; we call upon Your name,
declare Your wonderful deeds.*
Psalm 75:2

The Master's Telephone

When you need someone to talk to
But you find friends are away,
Or their lines are always busy
Tho' you try and call all day…

And you sit there feeling lonely,
Wishing you could reach a friend
Just to share some troubled thoughts
With one on whom you can depend.

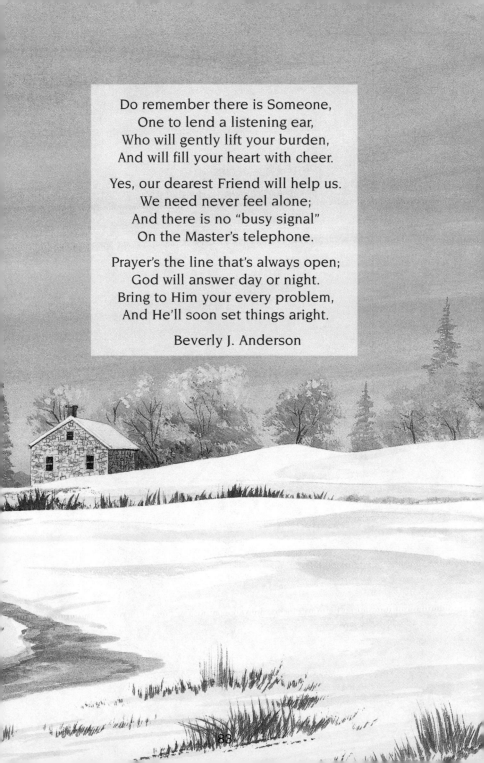

Do remember there is Someone,
One to lend a listening ear,
Who will gently lift your burden,
And will fill your heart with cheer.

Yes, our dearest Friend will help us.
We need never feel alone;
And there is no "busy signal"
On the Master's telephone.

Prayer's the line that's always open;
God will answer day or night.
Bring to Him your every problem,
And He'll soon set things aright.

Beverly J. Anderson

I am the vine, you are the branches. Whoever remains in me and I in him will bear much fruit, because without Me you can do nothing.
John 15:5

Serenity

Just give me some time in my garden;
There all my troubles to free.
For when I am there in my garden,
I am ever so near, Lord, to Thee.

I can see all the wonders of living
As the rich soil I sift through my hand.
And I watch as the seeds become blossoms,
Then bear their fruits from the land.

Just give me some time in my garden,
Some quiet time to spend alone.
For when I am there in my garden,
I am calm deep within, and at home.

Ruthmarie Brooks Silver

*The trees of the field shall bear their fruits, and the
land its crops, and they shall dwell securely on their
own soil. Thus they shall know that I am the Lord
when I break the bonds of their yoke and free them
from the power of those who enslaved them.*
Ezekiel 34:27

Friendship

I asked the Lord to show me faith
And He led me to you,
A Christian strong with kindness pure
That shows in all you do.
I asked the Lord to give me hope
And once again I found
The life you live a testament,
In patience hope abounds.
I asked the Lord to show me love
As He meant it to be,
And I saw love that's pure and true
In your life plentifully...
So now I think of you each day,
In every trial I face.
I meditate on your strong faith
And hold the Hand of Grace.
I have the hope that once was lost,
For now I see His love
That's true and pure and ever near
From Heaven's heights above.

Lynda Bryan Davis

One thing I ask of the Lord; this I seek: To dwell in the Lord's house all the days of my life, to gaze on the Lord's beauty, to visit His temple.
Psalm 27:4

He Is Always There

He is in the roaring thunder
And in the crashing waves.
Through all the storms of life
His is the Hand that saves.
Most times He's not so obvious,
He seems distant and so still.
But if you listen quietly,
He will give your heart its fill.
You may not always find Him,
But His eyes are set on you.
He keeps you in His constant care;
His heart follows what you do.
Don't worry if you can't see Him
When your life is caving in,
Or shout and hear no answer
And you think you cannot win…
He will come when least expected,
In a time that's all His own.
You will think He's left you stranded
And you're standing all alone.

Do not doubt Him for a moment,
For He has known all along
When and where you'll need Him
And His heart is never wrong.
He will come at the last second
When you think you cannot stand.
You will turn to hear a whisper
And reach out and find His hand.
You'll never understand Him –
That was never meant to be.
You must teach your heart to trust,
For no one is as wise as He.
He will surely answer you;
All His promises are kept.
Though you won't hear Him coming…
He comes on silent footsteps.

Marilyn Healey

When I Meet My Savior

Praise be to the Lord on high,
To Him whose Name is great!
Oh, that I could see His face –
It's so very hard to wait!

But soon there'll come a day when
My joy shall be complete –
I'll wake in Heaven's glory
And my loving Savior meet.

My tears of joy will overflow
When once our hands shall touch.
And I'll sing praise to Jesus,
The Savior I love so much!

Denise A. DeWald

90

Walk With Jesus

God knows our every weakness;
He knows our every fault.
In sinful situations,
Our hearts become distraught.
Worldly pursuits lead us
Foolishly down an empty road,
Keeping us imprisoned,
Carrying a heavy load.
Escaping through false pleasures
Give us happiness for a while,
But when we walk with Jesus,
We can conquer any trial.

Gloria A. DeWald

*So, as you received Christ, Jesus
the Lord, walk in Him.*
Colossians 2:6

Give praise for His mighty deeds,
praise Him for His great majesty.
Psalm 150:2

Don't Wait

Don't wait 'til you're needing a blessing
Because you've a burden to bear –
Turn to Your heavenly Father
And put all of your heart in a prayer.

Turn to Him in your gladness
When everything seems all right;
Praise Him for all of His goodness
That made your world so bright.

He deserves much more than our sorrows
That often we lay on His breast –
He's deserving our sincerest praises
And all in our lives that is best.

Rachel Hartnett

A Cup of Friendship

A cup of friendship from the heart
To let you know I care;
A simple gesture just for you…
A cup of love to share.

A touch of hope, a bit of cheer,
A prayer that you would know
Just how much you mean to me
Before you have to go.

A promise that we'll stay in touch
And visit now and then…
A cup of friendship from the heart –
A smile for you, my friend.

Jill Lemming

Be he rich or poor, his heart is content,
and a smile is ever on his face.
Sirach 26:4

The Melody of Spring

A carpet of green spreads over the valley
While snow lingers high on peaks.
A flower tentatively opens its petals,
Absorbing the sunlight it seeks.

New calves are frolicking down in the meadows;
Hungry hawks are surveying the fields.
Migrant ducks fly in from far away places,
Answering the call to which all Nature yields.

Rivers are rising with new-melted snow.
Leafless trees feel a stirring within.
Gardeners are carefully turning the soil
For the planting that soon will begin.

Throughout creation life is bursting with joy,
Inviting all Nature to sing
In sweet harmony, for we are all one
When we join in the melody of Spring.

Alora M. Knight

The flute and the harp offer sweet melody, but better than either, a voice that is true.
Sirach 40:21

Let There Be Music

Lord, let there be music to fill all my days,
Songs all around me to brighten my ways,
The rippling gurgle of clearwater streams,
And the whispering winds to accompany my dreams.

Put in my heart the song of blue skies,
And the symphony felt in a lovely sunrise.
In the exquisite tones of a pine forest's sigh,
Make me aware that Heaven is nigh.

The melody heard in a little child's voice
Can make the choirs of Heaven rejoice,
And the frollicking, trilling songs of the birds;
The music I hear in soft-spoken words.

Let me feel the crescendo an orchestra brings,
And the soft, soft tones of the violin strings.
The bold, thrilling notes of a big marching band
Shout love of our country all over the land!

As long as I live, Lord, let me sing;
Let the world around me in harmony ring.
And when on God's earth I no longer can roam,
Send thousands of angels to sing me on home!

Margaret Barkley Johnson

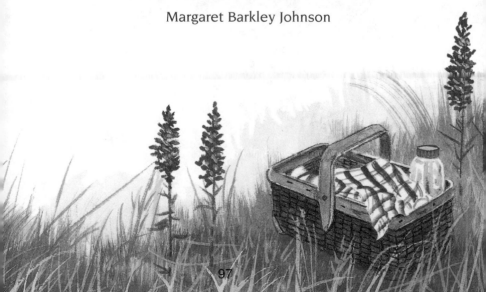

Welcome one another, then,
as Christ welcomed you,
for the glory of God.
Romans 15:7

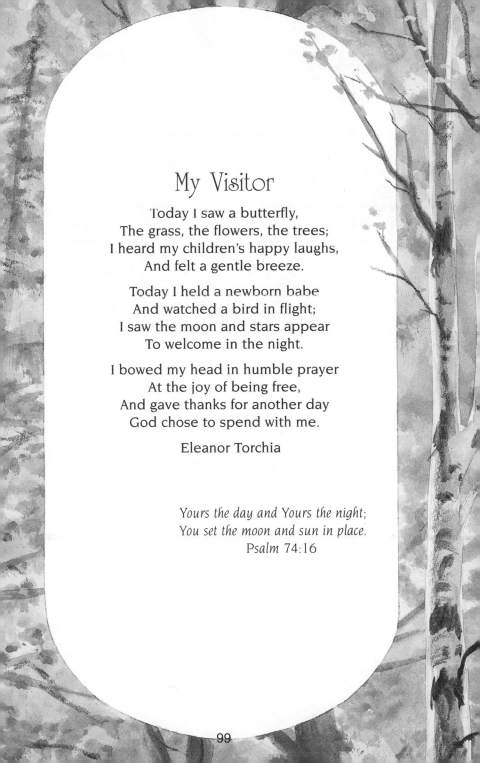

My Visitor

Today I saw a butterfly,
The grass, the flowers, the trees;
I heard my children's happy laughs,
And felt a gentle breeze.

Today I held a newborn babe
And watched a bird in flight;
I saw the moon and stars appear
To welcome in the night.

I bowed my head in humble prayer
At the joy of being free,
And gave thanks for another day
God chose to spend with me.

Eleanor Torchia

Yours the day and Yours the night;
You set the moon and sun in place.
Psalm 74:16

A Willing Vessel

What am I holding back from God?
Am I afraid to give my all?
Do I hide in the background?
Am I afraid that I might fall?

Lord, I need the courage
To live my life for You
And reach out to all I meet,
And do what I can do.

Dear Father, make me a willing vessel
That You can work through,
And as I reach out in love,
I give all the glory to You.

Dona M. Maroney

Rejoice

God's voice can calm each storm-tossed sea
And soothe each heart and soul;
When doubts sweep over me,
He bids faith take control.

He safely keeps tomorrow's keys
And hears our every prayer;
Each rugged path I know He sees
And walks beside us there.

Rejoice! Rejoice, my soul, rejoice
And all God's goodness tell.
He whispers, "Peace," and troubles cease…
God knows and all is well.

Phyllis C. Michael

Glory in His Holy Name; rejoice,
O hearts that seek the Lord!
1 Chronicles 16:10

A Smile

A smile is such a fleeting thing –
It comes and goes at will.
We never think what it conveys
Or what it can fulfill.

It is the language of the soul;
It's meaning knows no bounds.
It conjures up a friendliness,
On any earthly grounds.

It adds a grace to any life,
No matter what the day.
When joy or sadness do prevail,
It seems to light the way.

To share the bitter or the sweet,
With others it depends
On how a warm, encouraging smile
Can make us real good friends.

Yes, life can be much sweeter
If we would use its power,
For young or old it lends a charm…
It sweetens every hour.

Marion Pearl Crocker

God Opened Heaven's Windows Today

God opened Heaven's windows today
And sent His sunshine my way.
For when we're discouraged and blue,
Our Heavenly Father knows what to do
To lessen our load and cheer our heart;
Sweet merciful grace He doth impart.
His loving presence gladdened my day
And chased all my sadness away.
For when we're disheartened with care,
Our Comforter knows what burden we bear;
In loving compassion He fills our need
And stays by our side, our Friend indeed.

Kathryn Thorne Bowsher

The Treasure In My Soul

I have a treasure in my soul,
That God has given me.
A blessing that I would not have,
But for His grace, you see.
It came one day upon my being,
When all my world seemed dim,
I heard the knock upon my door,
And asked my Savior in.
I have a wonder in my soul,
A special joy each day,
A gift of life from Jesus Christ,
Who came to light my way.
This treasure, oh, this treasure,
'Tis buried deep within,
And I am rich beyond belief,
For I've placed my trust in Him.
His love and gentle guidance,
Will surely make me whole,
And within this lies the secret
Of the treasure in my soul.

Carol Steyaert

*For where your treasure is,
there also will your heart be.*
Luke 12:34

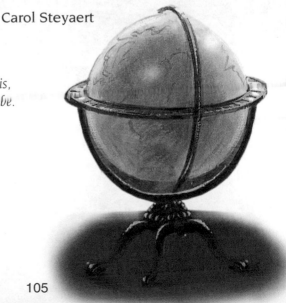

You visit the earth and water it, make it abundantly fertile. God's stream is filled with water; with it You supply the world with grain. Thus do You prepare the earth. You adorn the year with Your bounty; Your paths drip with fruitful rain.
Psalm 65:10, 12

God's Bountiful Blessings

Autumn days shine forth in bounty;
Nature's gifts come from the sod.
With the harvest comes rich blessings
And we kneel in thankfulness to God.

God sends the glorious splendor
Of our treasured Autumn scene;
Golden corn and waving wheat
With frost-nipped fields swept clean.

Beyond broad, misty meadows
Etched in hushed serenity,
Pillared oak trees laced in silver
Shine in resplendent artistry.

God's joyous and most precious gifts
Are those things we cannot see;
They span the universe to link
God's love and hope eternally.

Elisabeth Weaver Winstead

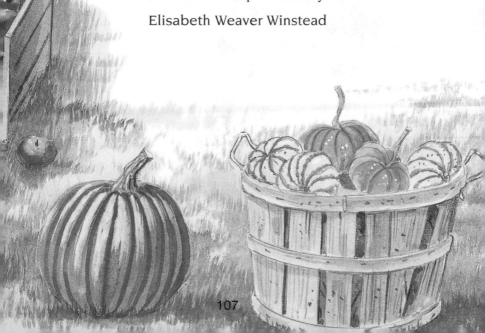

Peace I leave with you; My
peace I give to you; not as the
world gives, do I give to you.
Let not your heart be troubled,
nor let it be fearful.
John 14:27

Hope

Sometimes it seems we're always chasing
Rainbows way out there,
Sudden bits of sunshine
And the ever-evasive prayer.

Yet if we could only cherish
The moments God has given,
Simple, happy pleasures,
The honest joy of living,
Perhaps we'd find the answer is
For all of us to know:
Chasing rainbows in the sky
Will only stop the flow.

How sad is the illusion
That joy is way out there.
When if we silently listen,
We will find our peace in prayer.

Edna Louise Gilbert

Be strong and take heart,
all you who hope in the Lord.
Psalm 31:25

"Come to Me, all you who labor and are burdened, and I will give you rest."
Matthew 11:28

A Prayer Away

Each life must have its ups and downs –
The valleys and the peaks –
And trouble comes to one and all,
If rich or poor or meek.

But God will give the strength we need
For trials that come our way,
If we will only go to Him
And humbly kneel and pray.

"Cast your burdens on Me
And I will give you rest…"
This is the promise our Lord gives
To help us pass life's tests.

When you are feeling all alone
And troubles on you weigh,
Remember there's one who'll help you…
He's just a prayer away.

Kay Hoffman

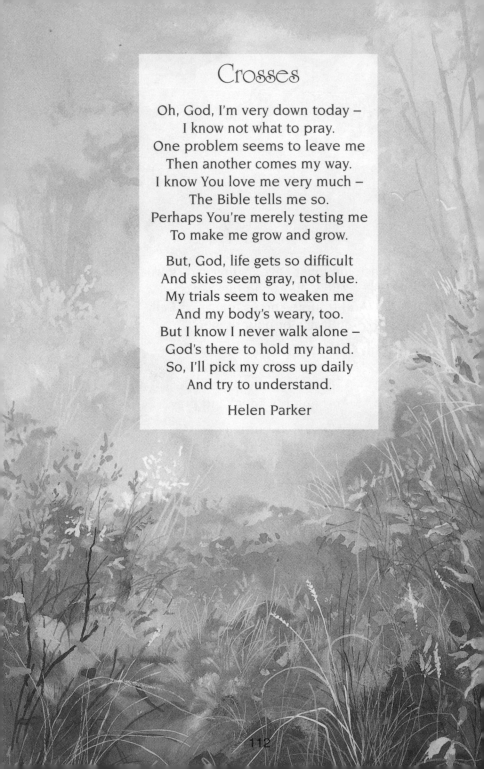

Crosses

Oh, God, I'm very down today –
I know not what to pray.
One problem seems to leave me
Then another comes my way.
I know You love me very much –
The Bible tells me so.
Perhaps You're merely testing me
To make me grow and grow.

But, God, life gets so difficult
And skies seem gray, not blue.
My trials seem to weaken me
And my body's weary, too.
But I know I never walk alone –
God's there to hold my hand.
So, I'll pick my cross up daily
And try to understand.

Helen Parker

Give Us This Day

Lord Jesus, give us courage
As we start out each new day
To fight off all temptations
That could cause Your child to stray.

Repair our damaged armor,
Let Your spirit fill our heart,
And know You will always guide us;
From our side You ne'er will part.

With Your hand in ours, dear Jesus,
We can make it through this life,
'Til at last You call us homeward,
Casting out our worldly strife.

Albert N. Theel

*Give us each day our
daily bread.
Luke 11:3*

'Til I Reach Heaven's Door

I want to be like You, Lord,
In all I do and say;
I want to be like You, Lord,
And serve You every day.

I want to show compassion
To all along life's way;
I want to love You dearly;
Oh, help me, Lord, I pray.

I want to seek the lonely
And those who are distraught;
I want to share with others
The many things You taught.

I want to run life's race well,
Be faithful to the end;
I yearn to be like You, Lord,
My Savior and my Friend.

And that I may be like You,
Thy mercy I implore
To keep me ever pure, Lord,
'Til I reach Heaven's door.

Loise Pinkerton Fritz

Golden Memories

Gone the hummingbird and firefly,
The morning glory climbing high...
Gone the magnolia from the tree,
Rose bouquets I picked for thee...

Gone too the crickets' choir
That entertained at the twilight hour...
Gone are geese and the butterfly
Wherever greener pastures lie...

Gone the robin's morning flight
And honeysuckle-scented nights...
Gone is Summer like a prayer
Without a trace in Autumn's air...

Gone like children out to play
Is each golden Summer day...
Flown like kites in the breeze
To be enshrined as memories!

Clay Harrison

He Knows Best

We learn the value of each day;
Sometimes, it's in a painful way,
For God alone still holds the key
To what is best for you and me.

It's hard to know just how to pray;
God understands each word we say.
It may make sense and it may not;
He fills the blanks when we cannot.

"You are My child," He whispers low,
"I'm with you everywhere you go…
I'll help to make your heartache cease
And grant you everlasting peace."

Anna M. Matthews

Learn to savor how good the
Lord is; happy are those who
take refuge in Him.
Psalm 34:9

A Prayer of Thanks

Lord, thank You for the sunshine
That brightens up my day.
Thank You for the storms of life
That sometimes come my way…
Thank You for each trial and test
That brings me to my knees,
And helps me grow stronger knowing
You'll meet my every need!
Lord, thank You for friends and loved ones
I cherish and adore;
The precious time we've shared together
Will in my heart be stored…

Thank You for the good times,
The heavy and the sad,
For all have worked together
For my good to make me glad!
Lord, thank You for the healings
When no other way was found…
Your miracles have touched my life
And turned it all around.
Thank You for all nature,
The very air I breathe,
All of Your marvelous creations –
The mountains, sky and seas,
Each flower in its beauty
Swaying gently in the breeze…
Everything beautiful to enjoy
Was made 'specially for me.

Millie Torzilli

Holy Father

Father, let us ask in prayer
For Thy will to be done.
I come to Thee in spirit and truth
And pray that we'll be one.
We honor Thy Son, Jesus Christ,
And in Him we believe.
This is why we have the faith
That from Thee we receive.

Carol Zileski

Haven

No matter what the case may be,
Though seeming without hope,
The light shines through, for God I see;
I know that I shall cope.

Encumbered with life's heavy weights,
I just can't keep on going.
But then I see the Lord awaits
To ease my troubles growing.

Once I give it all to God,
My woes just all escape me.
I look to Heaven, give a nod,
And pray, "Oh, God, praise Thee!"

The haven that's the God I know
Is always there forever.
His love just always overflows;
He'll never leave us... never!

Rosemary Gaines

*The Lord is my strength and my
shield, in whom my heart trusted
and found help. So my heart rejoices;
with my song I praise my God.*
Psalm 28:7

God Helps Those
Who Help Themselves

There is a tendency, it seems,
Amid each day's confusion
For man to mask frustration
In a sphere of grand illusions.
Instead of positive reactions,
He gets lost in fantasy,
Deluded in his daydreams,
Avoiding life's reality.
He spends each day expecting
Miracles to come his way...
Without extending effort
To make a fruitful day.

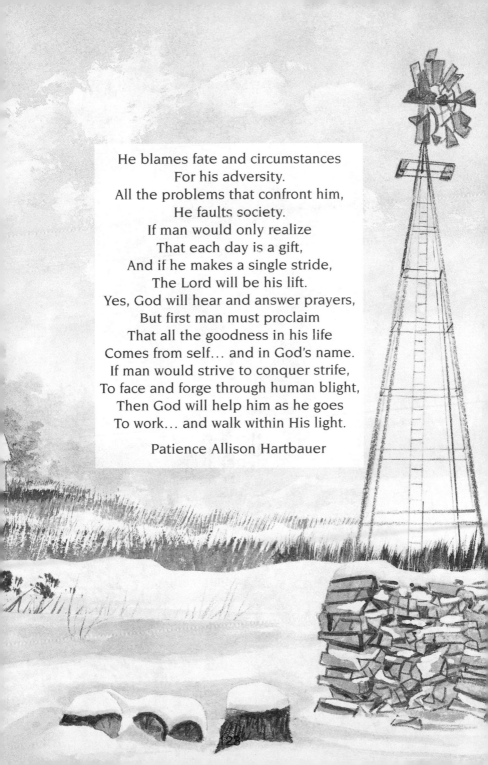

He blames fate and circumstances
For his adversity.
All the problems that confront him,
He faults society.
If man would only realize
That each day is a gift,
And if he makes a single stride,
The Lord will be his lift.
Yes, God will hear and answer prayers,
But first man must proclaim
That all the goodness in his life
Comes from self… and in God's name.
If man would strive to conquer strife,
To face and forge through human blight,
Then God will help him as he goes
To work… and walk within His light.

Patience Allison Hartbauer

The Grieving

When sorrow overwhelms your day
And your heart is filled with tears,
Go to God to ease the pain
Of the loss of one so dear.
He'll hold you in His heavenly arms
And comfort you with love,
And you will feel the healing warmth
That comes from Heaven above.

Dolores Karides

Thank-You Note

I tried to make a total list
Of all God's gifts to me,
But I soon stopped because I saw
It went on endlessly.

The gifts He gives are many more
Than I could ever say.
His love as well cannot be bound,
And guides me every day.

I also know that blessings come
Not just with joy and gain;
At times quite unexpectedly
They're part of trial and pain.

I need to have an open heart
Whatever life may bring.
Oh, let me magnify the Lord
And let my praises ring!

Amy C. Ellis

*At dawn let me hear of
Your kindness, for in You
I trust. Show me the path
I should walk, for to You
I entrust my life.*
Psalm 143:8

My Twilight Years

Oh, what a happy time of life,
These twilight years of mine.
I view things somewhat differently
Than in the years I've left behind.

Delight is found in simple things
That were taken for granted in the past.
I've heard it said throughout my life
That the best is saved for last.

I feel that I am more mellow
And now listen to others more.
I have a lot of time on my hands,
More than I ever had before.